Clearly You Are ESL

Ranjani Murali

The (Great) Indian Poetry Collective

Acknowledgements

An early draft of this book was submitted as my MFA thesis and remains at Fenwick Library at George Mason University, for which I will be grateful always to my professors Susan Tichy, Sally Keith, Jennifer Atkinson and Eric Pankey. After I came to the Mason MFA program, I experimented with form, structure, and collage in ways that I could not have imagined before. For the gift of postmodern poetry, I thank these wonderful people, particularly Susan and her "Book Beasts" course, as well as my peers in the program.

My family and friends, both in India and Fairfax, were a constant source of support. Not many people have seen this book in its current format, but to those who have—particularly Ellen, Minal, and Shikha, the founders of The (Great) Indian Poetry Collective, and Vidhu, my immediate editor who has provided insightful and supportive comments throughout—I am indebted.

I extend my gratitude to Sarah Evelyn Castro for transforming my manuscript into a beautifully designed book with a gorgeous cover.

Arjun, thanks for pushing me to submit this book, dear heart-twin. Sharanya, you were always here when I needed assurance and support, for which I will forever be in your debt.

To the editors of the following journals and platforms, where revised or previous versions of these poems have appeared, been displayed, or are forthcoming at the time of publication, thank you for putting some of these earliest experiments into print/the online ether: Susan Tichy & *Fall for the Book*: "Eye Prints" (exhibited at the festival); *Cricket Online Review & The Moment of Change* (an anthology of speculative poetry edited by Rose Lemberg): "Chants for Type: Skull Cap Donner at Center One Mall;" *The Alipore Post*: "a pad is a personal hygiene product like latex gloves;" *The Bombay Literary Magazine*: "Picked up Episodes" (published under the title "Picked Up Ghazals"); *Poetry at Sangam*: "Workbook Cursieve II," "How to Read Diaspora Cough Formula" and "Chants for Type: Beamboy Watching Cartoons in Five-Star Hotel Room Eating Ice-Cream;" *Nether Quarterly*: "Subvertisement: Ladies, please (phrases)" and "Beach Violations."

Contents

Part One

Define: Identify, or, Several Short Sentences for Our Language   1

Watchman   2

Workbook Cursieve I   3

Two Corruptions of the Ballad of Bappi Lahiri   5

Found: A Marriage Proposal, Webringtogether.com   7

Dear Offshore or Non-native Employee   8

Tourist Notice   10

Eye Prints, or How to Protest Want   12

Catalog of Pronouncements and Observations
Related to Ellis Road Eateries and Vendors   17

Part Two

Define: Dialect, or Winnowing Through   21

Chants for Type: Skull Cap Donner at Center One Mall   22

How the Webs Came to Be or Impending Verse Dedications to Rajinikanth   24

Workbook Cursieve II   26

Yama's Buffalo Halted and   28

Beach Violations   29

Discrishun   30

List of Communicable Moral Disease Clichés
Culled from Renegade Communist Hero Characters   36

Part Three

Define: Ladyspoke, or Ladies of Leisure Speak for All   39

Picked Up Episodes   40

Landing   46

How to Read Diaspora Cough Formula   47

a pad is a personal hygiene product like latex gloves   50

Subvertisement: Ladies, please (phrases)   52

Rushed Letter from East Asian Paradise for Single Male Journalist   53

Mariaatha   54

Chants for Type: Beamboy Watching Cartoons in
Five-Star Hotel Room Eating Ice Cream   56

Clearly You Are ESL: Workbook Cursieve III   58

Notes   60

Part One

Define: Identify, or, Several Short Sentences for Our Language

Ours is a lyrical language. A classical springing forth of reticent consonants. Our vowels are edged with wholesome clarified dissent. Our faces contort into melting plastic wires. When the state stamps our petitions with yes, we will eat our paper. Then, our hairy-eared clerks will turn. Singing roadside percussionists will turn. The streets lined with silver anklets will turn. The jasmine sellers' calls will turn. The last bell of the primary schools will turn. Our smithies and our firing coals will turn. Our paper words will turn, turn into the plastic horizon, all our sentences singeing at the corners.

Watchman

When I first went to sell Cancercure at Teynampet, the watchman smiled at me. His face was pitted with small-pox scars and his upper left canine was missing. *How are you madam*, he asked, scratching his ear. I took the elevator to the fourth floor but it stopped at the third. When I got off, I noticed that the walls were made of rice flour and the entire floor reeked of something arcane. I went looking for the stairs and found an ayah sitting with a basket full of dried fish and a broom made of palm leaves. *Come*, she said, *I am looking for Kovai Sarala's neighbor who buys my fish to make Kongu meen curry every Monday.* I held her hand, which felt like coconut shavings, and we walked down. The second floor smelled like a musty box office. *You know*, ayah said, *when your son becomes a man, you must hold a red chili over the fire until it browns and then circle it over his head else the ghostwomen get attracted to him.* When we came to the first level, she threw her broom away, saying *where the scent of this thing wafts, we can leave a broom to help ward off the small devils.* When we came to the lowest level, ayah removed her glass bangles and put them in my palms. I remembered watching the film Kanchana, where the transgender ghost likes to play dress-up with Sarala's things. As I pressed my fingers around the bangles, the watchman emerged, his cane raised, and began to whip my legs. *Stop, stop*, I screamed, *I just came to sell the latest brand of anti-carcinogenic medication made exclusively for all ladies.* He paused and pulled out a beedi tucked behind his ear. *Got a light, then?* When I offered him my lighter and the pale green edge of the beedi glowed a deep orange, he nodded his head. *I can tell from your twelve-o'clock shadow*, he said. He blew a stream of thin smoke. When I shuffled to readjust my dupatta, he smiled at me and offered me a beedi. *No commission*, he said, *for you.*

Workbook Cursieve I

There is a bull.

_____.

It has a big head.

_____.

You have bullets in your bag.

_____.

The bull is looking at your bag.

_____.

Your bag is orange.

_____.

You are peeling an orange.

_____.

Your friend throws away the peels.

_____.

The bull sniffs at the peels.

_____.

Your friend is looking at the bull.

_____.

The bull kicks its heels.

_____.

Orange peels are lying at your heels.

_____.

Your friend is lying.

_____.

There is a gun in his head.

_____.

Two Corruptions of the Ballad of Bappi Lahiri

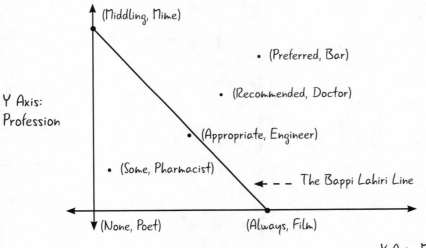

Y Axis: Profession

(Middling, Mime)

• (Preferred, Bar)

• (Recommended, Doctor)

• (Appropriate, Engineer)

• (Some, Pharmacist)

← – – The Bappi Lahiri Line

(None, Poet)   (Always, Film)

X Axis: Marriageability

Average Respectability Ratio; Indian Males; 16–35; Scale Undecided

And when Mithun moved
     his lips to flashing speckles bouncing
off shimmering skirts of pale-skinned girls,

I remember the man behind us
     whistled—a shrill savoring
of cigarette smoke and the renegade.

He was probably a BA working
     as an underpaid peon in Churchgate,
who ate *poha* for breakfast. And lunch.

On Sundays, he may have stood
            for hours outside film city in Bandra
waiting for Mithun Da to flash a boot,

a new patent leather jacket,
            or even a new silver headband
that he would later fashion out of star-shaped sequins,

bought at Rustom's Fancy Shop in Colaba market,
            and a plain white elastic band.
He may then have stitched each silver

sequin onto the cloth, and then slipped
            on his creation, the same stars
fanning into a new weave.

Found: A Marriage Proposal, Webringtogether.com[*]

an architect by passion and profession. ain't to accept mere existence. so trying to live a meaning
and cause, than just exist! not complex...am little composite...with intents...on work [with flare]
life [with flare] etc. open yet sensible. ain't basic but certainly do not subscribe swankiness too!
if interesting lets share mind...shall check if we work well! need a vibrant...witty,
open minded and creative, family loving...so if your it as said lets give it a shot!

---

[*]   Source: Online matrimonial advertisements, circa 2007-08

Dear Offshore or Non-native Employee

We must, in lieu of being
an internationally reputed
commodities exchange and trading establishment,
caution you that the following activities, not all
of which comprise an exhaustive list,
are to be henceforth impermissible and may constitute possible
grounds for termination of contract:

wearing handspun or ethnic attire;
carrying metal lunchboxes;
installing idols in the workspace (exceptions include replicas of superiors or Latter-day Saints);
wearing open shoes or shorts, even in May;
using non-mandatory symbols of religious affiliations on your person (including anklets);
using other languages during work hours as enforced by the meter in the bathroom, lunch room, and on your laptops;
                (a list of permissible English dialects is, however, available at the Human Resources Office);
utilizing more than an hour for lunch, bathroom breaks, or for walking between meetings;
eating without metal cutlery or instruments;
possessing decals or bumper stickers on your car that are unrelated to work or our brand; (the sticker may,
                however, carry an inscrutable yet common saying such as "work is worship," provided it is in English);
not responding to a fellow worker's sneeze with "God bless you;"
appropriating any office supplies or materials, including shredded paper for children's school projects;

installing colorful decorations in/on and musical reverse tunes for your cars;
carrying any paan or dried/fresh vegetation (plants, flowers or leaves) on your person or briefcase;
performing local religious rituals in the premises that involve the use of astrology or forecasting
                (Linda Goodman's thoughts on the Mercury retrograde are permissible; however, no color-throwing,
                cracker-bursting, bovine-based celebrations are allowed, though Christmas parties and St. Patty's day
                binge-a-thons like those in the Manhattan office are not only permissible, but strongly encouraged);

expressing disapproval against business or recreational practices of our head office, including the annual golfing tournament and bring-your-gluten-free-pet-to-work-day;

greeting colleagues with non-secular phrases such as "may the Pastafarian Goddess Supreme Shaman be with you;"

perpetrating idolatrous or frivolous dashboard culture;

and, of course, using the r-word (r*cism).

Tourist Notice

I.

Please watch your electronic items, your wallet,
your passport, your breasts, your edibles,
your laptop cases, the nape of your neck,
your Barnes & Noble gift cards, your frosty lipstick,
the small of your back and the line of your spine,
your sneakers, your stilettos, your evening shoes,
your morning after pills, your Advils,
your breakfast bars with a low glycemic index,
your pale freckled arms, your outlet mall bags,
your super-absorbent tampons, your vegan
gummy bears, your grapefruit gum.

II.

We are asking you not to stand in
line but to fan out into the line. Ours
is an egalitarian society; we believe
that everyone must approach from sameness,
stand with the line, rather than in line.
If you want coffee, please ask thrice,
and mention you do not want milk
because we are a nation of dairy
connoisseurs. We bathe our newborns
in milk and cream and swathe our
brides in milk-drenched silks,
our dead in milk-white shrouds.

If you think that women can wear pants,
we will agree most amicably, but please
don't rub the back pockets of your tapering
jeans when you wish to stretch or arch
your back. It is obscene and may invite a man
to stroke it. Then, you must not claim that he
is bumping into you everywhere
because we agree. He is.

Eye Prints, or How to Protest Want

Anything may be turned to one's advantage and profit; it is like the true alchemy by which all the bodies of nature may be turned to one's profit, by which even from poisons their most subtle elements may be drawn to produce the most salutary remedy for man...Have salt, but bring a little pepper. A pigeon, an artichoke, a bottle of wine, a handkerchief. We want nothing that might have appeared in any other public sheet.

Where money? Daily you put water down land, keep tree digging in the land and how trees? A tree used to be herbal. Now you understand newsletter, citizen people who clicked like button for vote? After election and before heard news plague rat. Now came news swine flu, next come malaria control. Seen not poor people by the road. How call? Back go to Bihar, UP work at farmer, house building there. Government confess, give explanation!

Secondly, observe that although the dangers to the Fatherland may sometimes force a Nation to severe measures, it is also the proper dignity of a great people to exercise clemency; this, it seems, would be the case here, for conspiracy exists only in the imagination, and the great conspirator is a glass jar. You will now have been persuaded how certain persons, under the appearance of interest and service, have proved most false and cruel.

We are not responsible. Can't avoid dearth price punish law? From Minister notice, I have seen a letter. And have you looked birth-death department? I have experience birth-death certificate, but interrupt. Citizen people liked chewing tobacco, smoking cigarette, drink alcohol. Why punish less price? Who tease vote for? Can speech avoid news? Can't arrest? Break pledge? Have you seen read pledge? Dirty pledge? Like you love your country?

A strict, well-occupied life is the best protection against all these perils. A drainpipe serves as a speaking tube; the current of a stream brings letters in a clog, carrying the answers back when pulled by a string. Everybody has his own trestle bed and little mattress. Some cook and hang the leg of the lamb at the window to make it more tender, others have recourse to the perpetual soup pot. Everybody fraternizes. One's sleep is light when accompanied by such a thick knotted rope.

Come summer season, tree crush his leaves fallen under land, yellow color leaves. Summer burn fire point to earth, burn tree, volcano earth. Then rainy season, over sky come cloud dropped water under land. Winter season tree fallen not down land. Have you seen history story book? Now you see not past history book. You forgot history book. Now you see an environment. Now see...how see? Humility air, burning land volcano crowd near building house.

A few consolations...in a folded handkerchief, in a pigeon's beak, in the hem of a necktie. The Commission entrusted with the general supervision cannot but see all those who have had a hand in such particular plots. This makes supervision extremely laborious and a common sense of disorder prevails—a continual gathering of individuals whose whole existence is consumed in oaths against versifying, card-playing and music, not forgetting backbiting.

Over sky house standing building construction, down break. Down stand not tree. Come, burning fire humidity. Unfit body headache. Come drop not rain down city, away cloud out city, away cloud to sea, drop rain down, sea flow stormy enter to city, on the sea ice mountain, dissolve water flow more. Spit down, dirty city, from government buy product, cleaning machine, more buy medicine. Earth life air, wind, water, land, sky. Why change? How avoid? Can you break an earth?

...took part in that procession, that warlike march, falling into line, to faces that would not have laughed for an empire and all the more comic a sight in that light, handheld, coming from below, which seemed to smear with bistre all the salient points of the face and bring out only the staring eyes, all that jumble of darkness and light, of movement and repose... the doors closed by a simple latch.

There are countries stay his own citizen expect say beggar. They are living his election card. Daily day water pipe level flow to house at morning, night. And close flow water pipe level to house at afternoon, evening. How life year? Can't clean work, can't work an environment. Stop loss; stand tree air wind leaves humility air save payment. More water less earth come sweat. See green.

Catalog of Pronouncements and Observations
Related to Ellis Road Eateries and Vendors

Standard Biscuit Factory has the best donuts (the kind with jelly)
and the best paneer tikka wraps served with sachets of ketchup.

Saktivel and his friends frequently visited Mani's chai shop between 2005 and 2006
to catch a glimpse of four college girls who wore sleeveless shirts every day.

It is rumored that the biriyani that is served near the Amman temple on Saturdays
may contain cat or dog meat, though the anonymous donor denies it.

Mani's chai shop always has the crispest English-style vanilla biscuits in glass containers.
The last one is sold everyday at approximately 4:15 pm.

Poori-bhaji is served on steel plates in a shop opposite Kasturi building.
Chutney and sambar are served on request, but the owner is always out of vadas.

Khader bought a fresh goat from the butcher near Bukhari every Friday and waited
until its jugular vein was severed and the blood drained into the gutter full of bones and intestine.

The man who makes parottas near *Beauty Photos* always wears a grey vest;
his fingers are sleek and slick with oil as he folds every parotta exactly three times.

One Suppan sold guavas from a mobile cart every summer evening. He never told his customers
that their interiors were as pink as the flesh of a newborn, but he did put them in green plastic bags.

Natasha and her friends smoked only Goldflakes in the afternoons, blowing smoke hurriedly past the three men
in leather chappals who always stood at the entrance of the chai shop.

Once I asked for a dosa at SBF and the woman at the counter folded her eyebrows and said
the Saravana Bhavan is across the street, akka. Then she gave me a piece of guava cake to sample.

The large, rectangular stone sizzled and threw up steam whenever the parotta maker splashed
some water to test the temperature. I once asked him if he'd been scalded and he said *no, I know how hot the fire is.*

When I passed by a man in a white cap the third time in successive weeks, I asked him, *aren't you a Muslim? Why
are you standing next to the Amman temple?* He licked his fingers and said *biriyani is good, ma.*

One day Natasha and I were eating puris when she laughed and said that she had stubbed her cigarette on a
man's face because he said he loved her for wearing sleeveless shirts.

Suppan disappeared one evening after a girl died of food poisoning. I saw him at Mani's later, eating the last
vanilla biscuit and telling a young boy with a scar on his face that he would live

off temple biriyani now.

Part Two

Define: Dialect, or Winnowing Through

In Tamil, we challenge. In Hindi, we capitulate. In the doggerel Englishes, we conquest. Several days after the boards are passed, we celebrate the examination of the grammars by tearing apart our essay writing textbooks, divining our futures into the syllabus of emailed minimalism. Who tells our chasming registers apart, who knows why we splinter the vowels and mix up the v and w?

Chants for Type: Skull Cap Donner at Center One Mall

"if you want friendly mouth for that also you need money."
   —Reader Amrit Patel on comment board, Feb. 14, 2011, Rediff.com

(Repeat after me:)

Mouth has slick pools.

(Now repeat:)

Mouth has silk spools.

(Now I won't remind you, you do it.)

Mother has silk mouth. Feed milk sugar bride. Honey veil silk oh.

(Very good. Applause ensues.)

Feed mother, silk money, milk money mouth money.

(Very good. Applause ensues.)

Feed mother, silk money, milk money mouth money.

(Faint sound of electric train siren grating on wet autorickshaw mudflaps.)

Slick bride, sugar money find feed, veil silk, milk spill.

(Exposed armpits, hair slick along eustachian sweat-curves.)

Bride mother be find sweet silk. Sugar mother.

(Unknown audience member quotes film: "I have ma what have you," snaps fingers.)

Sugar mouth mother mouth oh money mouth silk mouth mouth mouth bride mouth.

(Hyundai Accent, plum red, automatic locks, spins on the podium, a buzz ensues. Buzz.)

Oh, sugar sugar veil. Money find feed honey mother money.

(Checkered flag mounted on coffee shop banner titled "Drink a Date with Aamir.")

(I'll help you sharpen polished little finger on cutlery if you keep going.)

(Pigeon flies in, lands on glass face of centerpiece eagle-beak.)

Mouth be bride?

(Trains leave every half-an-hour, relieving you of exposed car flaps).

How the Webs Came to Be or Impending Verse Dedications to Rajinikanth

I.
These are webs, spangled, broken

silk, pieces of filament strewn
over our tongues, the sibilance of

stemmed and spelt dissolving

the glottals, the pit of each stomach-held
consonant, the breath-ensconced vowels,

the *Shut up da somberi.*

II.
Along grey hallways are lit

particulate shapes, the pink shape of a "D"
from "Diverse Voices Amongst Us." Listen

is a form of see and pause

the first chai shop on Ellis Road bleeds a poster
for "Want to look like White," a translation of

Karuppu thaan yennakku pidicha...

III.
Along Anna Salai, faces agleam

with a shared classical tongue melt flash.
Hollowed out voices in the subway travel

to studios where negatives flush

with white. Lined eyes and zari emerge
from fade to luminous edges. The magazines call him

Thalaiva, Supershtar.

IV.

Meet the King aligned perpendicular

to the hand-waving, dark-haired life size
blowup, us the samplers of Mount Road

tributes, the splash of fluorescence

reflected in helmet visors, broken glass shards,
brown toddler-eyes, breaths held, lips cinched

at *Exclusive Interview da.*

V.

Beedi signals, symbols square—

we are confronters, we seek to redeem, we are upheld—
Long Live Classical Divine Tamil is a property, a fist-held hand-clasped

exhalation, an asking,

for space and for stand. The man in the corner shop
smokes rings, an ah, an aah, and a zh, not sanitized, but claimed, as in

Dai keLava.

Workbook Cursieve II

The little girl goes to school.

_____.

The teacher writes letters on the board.

_____.

The little boy carries a green bag.

_____.

The letters are white and round.

_____.

The birds chirp in the trees.

_____.

The girl draws a house with a door.

_____.

The teacher erases the letters on the board.

_____.

The boy draws a house with a dog.

_____.

The teacher opens the door.

_____.

The dog carries a bird in its mouth.

_____.

The girl erases the green trees.

_____.

The boy puts the dog in his bag.

_____.

The birds fly away.

_____.

Yama's Buffalo Halted and

I found him in a field of billowing
grass, stirring a pot of avial.

That which is succulent unfolds
the end, he said, cutting open

a sachet of coconut milk. Hand me a wok,
he gestured, his mouth full of pogaielai

spiked with cardamom fogging his
glasses, five strands settling on his cotton shirt.

When I picked up the brass wok, potatoes appeared
in it, already sautéed, sprinkled with freshly sliced

ears and fingertips. Must I eat this, I asked.
Why? He wiped the back of his hand on his apron,

ladled the avial and some Ponni No. 2 rice onto a plate
and pressed my right arm. The lotus stream

was tinged with beads of sweat. You cannot drink
on an empty stomach. Then he placed his palm

upon my head and I could see the counting
of each grain of rice, its white belly

sliced between my teeth, the words full
of the traces of husk.

Beach Violations

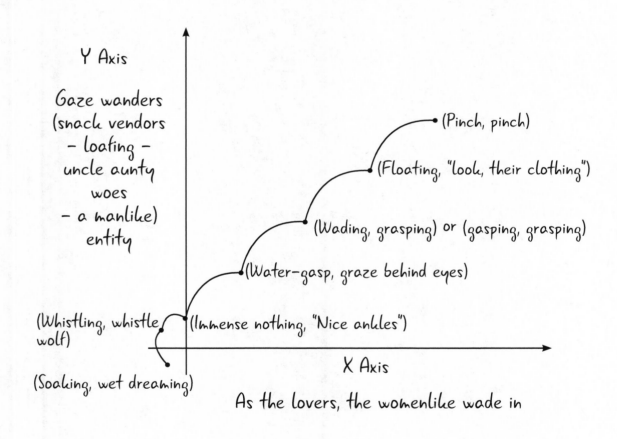

Y Axis

Gaze wanders
(snack vendors
– loafing –
uncle aunty
woes
– a manlike)
entity

(Pinch, pinch)

(Floating, "look, their clothing")

(Wading, grasping) or (gasping, grasping)

(Water-gasp, graze behind eyes)

(Whistling, whistle, wolf)

(Immense nothing, "Nice ankles")

(Soaking, wet dreaming)

X Axis

As the lovers, the womenlike wade in

Discrishun[*]

Introinduction, or "Acquisition of India"

written towards the end of invasion of conventional variety of transfer of kinship, this manual
is strange, very strange through might of silhouetted against a background of scandals, wars
and intrigues here too the reader will find the majesty of stride through centuries and dozens of others
daily bought and sold but it is designated for the strangest of all widespread rules of exchange

Key:

Situation
Suggested Response Unequivocal
Actual Response
Gandhian System Dictates Reasonably

---

[*]   This poem has been extensively collaged from the letters of MK Gandhi, as well as *Mayflower: A Story of Courage, Community and War* by Nathaniel Philbrick, and *The History of Islam* by Robert Payne.

Upon are indolent, luxurious, ignorant and cowardly beyond all conception bare men,
or "The Age of Clive"

In all situations concerning
       the society of my subjects especially
       the ladies, not one of whom is
       even decently approaches to exercise
       my authority with lest I should weaken my
       means if performing my
       public duty

For all
       impeach him in the name of people of under
       and whose human nature itself of both sexes
       into this closed circle, except by death

Yet

       as to render it improbably that they can be able
       for many years to come, to give
       any material disturbance to the British
       possessions are to be ceded to us

(And a aspirate Gandhi say:
the liberty to make native
recites of the same civil
discharged nation as an arbitrator.)

Upon is the strangest of all governments our Indian empire which shall not be strange, or "The Victories of Eyre Coote"

In all situations concerning
        is a body unfit for government
        are your loving friends
        based on trade inhabited by
        open to distraction little
        fitted for imperial functions

For all
        entrusted with the sovereignty of
        a large population close their
        commercial business: a vast country
        that empire has conducted

Yet
        one hundred millions people variously
        calculated our internal danger
        may involve our complete submission
        but what constitution can we give to our

(And a aspirate Gandhi say:
in his own right, and takes
it because he is a brother;
state it is not his act.)

Upon this mutual convulsion most revolting to their feelings, or "The Wellesleys"

In all situations concerning
        and a red glare the walls are going
        this is an awful hour, my darling
        of children's hands and feet permitted
        the retaking barrier being

For all
        as may hereafter be apprehended
        suits the occasion well and will be taken
        down for such deeds will be high
        up by the thigh exactly in front of no
        one spoke

Yet

        have ample force contemplated
        the destruction of their females
        while the cattle were running mad
        with thirst as a duty without discrimination

(And a aspirate Gandhi say:
humanly inclined people alive to their dumb
driven cattle and non-violence does not
require that passivity.)

Upon servants of the company accompanied with much liquid refreshment

In all situations concerning
        inside were much like home as possible
        cane chairs being gradually
        moved round to follow the shade
        in varying degrees of squalor
        with no concessions to tropical
        or sub-tropical conditions of
        the ceaseless floggings

For all
        to be made for the ungovernable passions
        contrived to live well admitted
        that no blame ought to be attached
        to a cursory debauch or applied their
        remedies of blooding, purging, must have
        vent in this stimulating climate

Yet
        pipe in mouth and lounged about
        wild local wenching were enabled
        to enjoy the pleasure of an
        English fireside on this side of eventual
        incapacitation and infirmity till years

(And a aspirate Gandhi say:
that make chimneys of their mouths
of public morality are statutorily
exempted a perfectly natural act.)

Upon rests our internal danger may involve our complete submission or "The Age of Reform"

In all situations concerning
        country, especially a wild
        opine into violent collision
        fully cognizant by homeless
        vagrant governing machines

For all
        imbecility, as ourselves
        vacated the field for civilian
        can do is impolitic throw their
        arms around them kiss them

Yet
        rose high and thick a strewed all
        spit at us fell into our glistening
        accoutrements masterly manner
        and shell a great stir of cold steel

(And a aspirate Gandhi say:
my dear idiots are mercenaries
British bayonets exist on British
sufferance heirs from running
mad inserted before civil.)

List of Communicable Moral Disease Clichés
Culled from Renegade Communist Hero Characters

paan and rotting wood (under the table) breath strappy heels (forsaking
the mellifluence of silver anklets) blatant toting of the flag or anthem at
film awards (so much for selling the country for a few shiny dancers
from modeling agencies) teaching children how to use computers (flowers
are anachronistic olfactory stimuli) throwing sickle or oxen for diesel
tractors and machetes for mammoth motors that drill borewells into a
rabbit's heart spurting red not water making cloth impermeable to bees
rain the patting of a ravi or seema at dinner and food an anomaly packed
into plastic no flesh to peel no semblance of erstwhile wholeness large
tomatoes hard enough to play cricket with smelling much like resin no
earth to take in and friends companions unions gatherings reeking of
silk kurtas and safari suits and a clean grey gandhi minted glossy like
the charkha gone forever like the ashoka chakra machine stamped with synthetic
ink to cover disemboweled jawans i knew as boys who were simply 24 gun salute
fond of the occasional old monk and rifle play instead of anvil and who
can blame them the smithies are only as hot as icarus flying taxes
into sky waiting for the anthem to save you where only a sickle suffices

Part Three

Define: Ladyspoke, or Ladies of Leisure Speak for All

When queued up, cut a sliver off this tongue pile. Toll violations spontaneously erupt where we perform our limerick of miso-gyny-trans-port-violence-fend-off-domestic-trangress-ions. We quickly glance over our shoulder. Some of them have left in airconditioned Volvo buses. Some have rigged the system. There is no we.

Picked up Episodes[*]

I'm going to quit school and join the boy scouts.

He ran away when he was fifteen. The sleeper trains used to have green leather seats.
The newsflash read: *Traps are being laid to capture innocent animals and enslave unsuspecting natives.*

When the lodge owner asked for his address, he walked out.
Outings during June were fantastic with a good strong swell and offshore winds. What more could we ask for?

The hotel owner said *we only offer room to married couples and families,* so we smiled and bought souvenirs.
Mahabali offered his head and then the universe was consumed.

An "invincible man," he is well loved as a god by the primitive tribes in the area.
We drove past Koovathur twice, with him insisting all the while that *I would give my head to live in this plot of land someday.*

Is Mahabali a real giant? Yes. He also eats babies.
He admitted later that he'd been ready to work as a tea boy near the station, as long as he did not have to pray on Fridays.

---

[*]   Collaged from dialogues of Full House, cross-searched on Google using Boolean and other methods.

A job is what you do to get free time.

There are three ways of getting to T. Nagar from Adyar.
When I came to the city, the Greams Road Fruit Juice Shop had only one branch: on Greams Road.

During the evening shift, there was only one guard at the door. Nirmala and I called him *Nepali baiyya*,
An essay to describe the non-dual transcendent basis of all existence.

When Mahabali returns, he will unseat Indra and turn the heavens over.
Once, when I was walking back home, a man stopped his motorbike and said *Sit, baby. Want a ride?*

I think of the power outages sometimes. We ate lots of Parle-G and wiped our foreheads with our dupattas.
Indira the maid was really named after Indira Gandhi or perhaps she was herself sickly.

Our boss said they had struggled to emerge as the pioneer in industry and sugarcane plantations.
And then it came to be that I always ordered the muskmelon special (without sugar).

It smells like family.

Appa goes for a walk every morning at six-thirty. The house is required to smell like Lizol before he leaves.
My neighbour has a dyslexic child. We played noughts and crosses.

Shiva holds the poison in his throat at Vellore. You can throw a coin into his mouth.
The exhibits encourage the building of strong social skills by creating situations that require children to work as a team.

No membership is required and all bookings are confirmed and guaranteed at Vellore youth hostels.
When we caught the watchman napping during a robbery, he said the saleswoman was nice to him.

My father spends Sundays counting all the loose change in the puja room. He plays Solitaire on the odd day.
Most people use aluminum coins unless they want to get their children married, in which case, silver is used.

I asked Indra where she got her perfume from. She always replied, *oh, my him, you know.*
When they shut off the power, I sat in the verandah making collect calls. Appa snored the whole time.

We will try not to smudge.

Our faces are painted in black kohl. We are lips, unlined.
Aachi masala—presidency is situated here. It has the perfect blend of homely aroma, so the marriage stays alive.

I was at home with my grandmother when the woman selling condoms asked to see my husband.
When Shakti revolted, Shiva destroyed her, because he was never one to stand disobedience.

I told her, *he is not here yet*. When my grandmother asked, I told her the woman was selling voltage adapters.
She was reincarnated anyway, because single Gods upset cosmological hierarchies.

My grandmother replied, *so what? The tv screen always goes blank just when the heroine is getting married. We could use them.*
Jalakantheshwara is a misnomer because Shiva's throat was full of poison, not hydroelectric charge.

On my last date, a man pulled up next to the car and said we were indecent.
My father, when told about the episode, said *these youngsters.*

Are we, like, together?

When my mother called, she expressed disgust over the quality of hair products. *No wonder everyone is uncoupling.*
24X7 was running an interview about seed saving, cultural security, and economic insecurity in India, denoting hope.

The inductive coupling process, the "antenna-like" circuits within, use an energy depleted world as their jumping off points.
My aunt called in exactly ten minutes to show me profiles of Asterisk and Reliabil_Man on Indianmatrimony.

It is imperative to maintain a genealogy directory of well-known and not-so-well-known family names to record more hits.
On the last date, he also assured me that the legality of non-matrimonial partnership would soon be validated by the judiciary.

Both Shakti and Aachi masalas are currently looking for a spice mixture that can be used to season anything, even milk bread.
Yet, I met Asterisk because Amma insisted that investment bankers whose last name was Kumar *keep their hair as they age.*

Are you familiar with the trend of historical prices, historical volume, splits and dividends, he asked.
The Supreme Court ruled that conjugal relationships did not have room for questions in order to hold in a court of law.

Picked up.

The authentic market focuses on us following the threads of our inner impulses.
Amma was horrified and kept saying that *looking on the internet doesn't mean you should lie and make things up.*

I told the doctor that I had fallen off the scooter on the way back from a business meeting. He frowned.
Brain imaging studies seem so simple and elegant: hook someone up to a functional MRI machine.

The first tv show I worked on was called *Business Hour*. Aachi's tender quoted better prices and we sold our breaks to them.
The MRI established that no serious injuries had been sustained. He kept frowning even then.

The imaging community has the best marketing exposure on the internet, coupled with color pictures of services and products.
Before I resigned, Human Resources was circulating a memo that read: *Wanna do your part?*

We could use whatever you can afford in this tender start-up phase: Donate here. Then, stay in the loop with us here.
Later, I overheard Dr. Kumar telling the intern: *I need to sneak away for a relaxing trip. I never meet single women with brain damage.*

Landing

At Peelamedu airport, the woman in the khaki pants looked at me with a twisting lower lip. Do you have any portable electronic items, she asked. Yes, I replied, though, they are mostly gifts for former lovers. She stepped closer and unzipped the sleeve running down my arm. You are not allowed to carry this through the scanner, she said, pulling out a boiled egg I carried because I had a protein deficiency. I saw her crush the egg between her fingers and her palm until the soft flesh split along the axis. Here, she said, holding up yellow-grey yolk as though she had harvested an oyster, eat it. I looked around at the gentleman in the grey safari suit and asked him to hold my electronic stilts. Then, I sat on the floor, cross legged, wiping my hands on my thighs. She handed the small crumbling glob and I put it in my mouth, pressing it down with my tongue instead of biting. I felt it stick to my teeth and tasted the stench of rusting metal. Swallow it, she said. I tried passing the goop through my throat, but the dry croissant I ate on the plane made its way up. As I vomited near her feet, the woman shook her head, turned to her colleague and said...maybe the shell cracked as it boiled.

How to Read Diaspora Cough Formula[*]

"Finally, to expel someone from the Disneyland club, accuse him repeatedly of trying to brainwash children with the doctrine of colorless social realism, imposed by political commissars."

-*How to Read Donald Duck: Imperialist Ideology in the Disney Comic,* Ariel Dorfman and Armand Mattelart, Trans. David Kunzle, 1975, Pg 26

it's Air India   honest Maharaja bowing   never a European geometric
          logo   skidding into
view righteous   fog of human breathing   flailing shirtless excitement below
          how much   nostalgia
packed into descent   from transatlantic   bleed-air oh there's a window
          with heroine   clad in sweatshirt
cocktail dress   *jing jang jing jang*   *cowgirl* the crew is dancing
          amassing   nods head bobs
trays of orange   juice gin bottle minis   sashaying to exit pulling lever
          slick   device
yielding crevice   into another threshold   no jet bridge but sharp stairway
          Pythagorean   hypotenuse
severe creaking   into tropical writhing   earth tarmacs always shell shocked
          crack   here
no luggage   is retrieved bargained for   foisted on cart no haggling with
          hands   seizing
fardel a direct   weaving through altercation   paraphernalia of salary slip/salaried sepoys
          ample   bellied
father is here *oho*   *oho precious jewel upon my* *crown of ecstatic barony emblem of unforetold*
          prosperity   *boyman*

---

[*]   Shake well horizontally and vertically before consuming.

awaits silver chariot   *no horse no wait oxen*   no that can't be oh yes a palatial enclave erected
               contains   *your lot*

smells of verdigris   line airport rails   *so lovely to breathe like this again daddy* she
               bronzes   lips in compact

case his straining to   contour   pronounced consonants produces stitches together
               an arc   of forehead

folds the French   eau de toilette is unsettling   forearms ebullient *this will not do* he tides over
               cloying   attention

to penury smoking   chaibiskutboy chicken   coops rattling in trucks hoardings with Boost
               fidgeting   encircled

by fatfatis hand   carts wheelbarrows   vintage helmets neon plastic cricket bats she
               delights   in swashbuckling

puppet song ice   cream man's bell strung   on cart but wait briefcases snap shut
               cool   slivers

of glass ripple across   umbrella points *hey hey*   *lady want some of me* tight t-shirt girl winks
               green   streaks

on jeans the girl   recoils what bucolic   noiselessness can pervade this shoreline
               rolling   by window

father smiles into   view *Oberoi Taj Treescape*   *International* tuxedoed man steps up nods
               bland   luxury

boots riddle her   jute seeking she is   capitulated into the wasteland of crystal
               Burma teak   frontispieced

interception so   much brass polish   the palate craves paper craves cotton
               deep   ensconced

efflorescing from   pods green as veins   on her covered breasts *oh dear* if the
               arranged   orchestrated

lifeplan includes   chandeliers who knows   if the mouth of the candelabra
               open   or shut

will flicker   like the braziers of Borivali   smithies in June smoke so
               thick   with brass

48|

the sputum   of hundreds shines on   their tongues assuages her
          sore   throat
caught from   plane disinfectant   and too much soap yes too
          much   *bucolic delight perfume*
she concedes   too much verdigris   and paper mill ramshackle
          blot   out puppetsong
and Pythagorean   hand cart leaning against   awning till the monochrome man
          rasps   *clear clear*

a pad is a personal hygiene product like latex gloves

How, I imagine, this memo could have read:

space out your thighs; you will be
searched. one of you almost tried to cram
your deodorant stick down the sink but we
fished it out. your uncle from the *gulf*
who liked to stroke your back bought
you the stiff toilet paper you tried to sneak
into the ladies' room. a ream of paper wedged
under my foot, that day unironed itself
into creases on every face i supervised. no
one told me there was shit plastered on
my soles, hardened, full of the fecund misgivings
the latex on the conveyors evades. but
this bleeding, it is unpardonable: an effluent
from your peasant-veins, your mocking,
warm hips, those pop songs you like to
play on your cheap korean mp3 players.

when i see your tears trickle down,
i will smear some toilet paper on them
and nod. the management prefers you
rinse and take it home: your modesty,
i mean. there are only so many doors
you can fumble shut before i
wipe away your smirk, your taut
petticoat strings, your my... please
didn't flush down madam please madam

50| *   Based on a news article on women in a mall in Kerala being strip-searched after a pad was found in the toilet.

Instead I saw you from the corner, writing

> quality control fail sample # 56.
> reason: uneven at palms; bad material. & no, i don't
> anticipate women holding placards
> outside wearing orange lipstick, saying fucking
> bourgeoisie, & interns, in a room somewhere,
> running ads for fair-forever running
> up to a supervisor, like me, exclaiming,
> let's send the CEO pads as a statement, no,
> till his mailbox overflows, while you fish out
> your underwear from a pile and i peel
> off the gloves i almost threw
> earlier into a pile of rejects.

I hum now (the song
on my headphones:) the ebb
of our shared shames, our bodies
in their familiar state, thrumming—
conveyors spinning toward, into, the promise of another, no prism
of shared phlebotomies, no cisterns cracked and patched, searched   without question,
without the trace   of wound.

Subvertisement: Ladies, please (phrases)

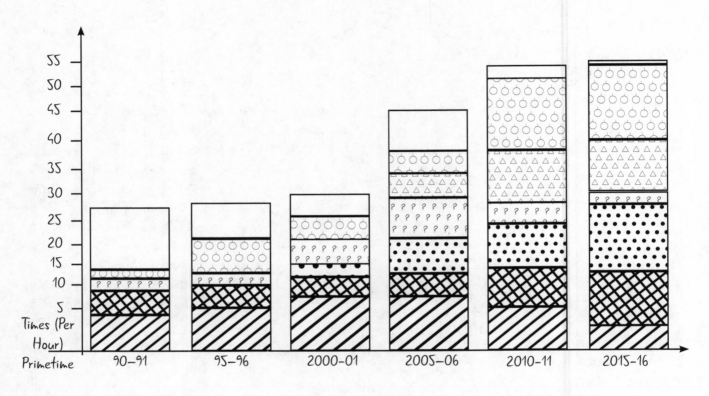

Times (Per Hour)

Primetime

90–91 95–96 2000–01 2005–06 2010–11 2015–16

Key

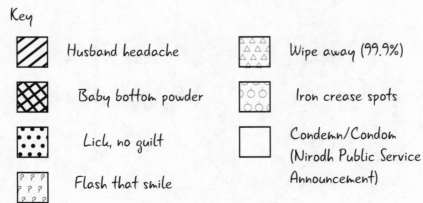

Husband headache

Baby bottom powder

Lick, no guilt

Flash that smile

Wipe away (99.9%)

Iron crease spots

Condemn/Condom (Nirodh Public Service Announcement)

Rushed Letter from East Asian Paradise for Single Male Journalists

Seriously machan, imagine that these
coconuts are green, like our school
uniform but the bit about breasts everywhere is exaggerated.
All droopy and shit. I mean this canned
coconut milk sours easily if you don't place it
in the windowsill in a dark pot
of water or beer. There's this large marble
statue of Buddha—he looks like he is
puking. The robe looks like it was stuck
to his thighs. Remember the full nights
in Goa da? Without that one in a sarong? Seriously,
my sandals are chipping. The sand is too
corrosive but yeah, the debris crack your heels.
I met this vellai journalist who eats oatmeal da
and he was livid when he was told
there were no microwaves.
I had to bloody read about the GDP to drown
out his screaming. But later he got struck—
wait, there's a phone call.
The minister—machan, he is serving rack
of lamb and food.

Mariaatha

In one stroke,
        brown
sweat striking

they felled her,
        flailing
words muffled, trussed

teeth. The gunny bag
        stained
dark, maybe even red,

dragged along. Falling
        light following,
they brought her out

to a cheap tape deck and stale toddy,
        to grunt and
straw thatch scratch. But

the altar in the hut, (it is
        said) blazed
and Mariaatha felled

in sparks bales of hay,
        reddening eyes;
fleeing was not considered.

When she returned to
       leaky roof
and slow-simmer kerosene stove,

they shivered, wiped their foreheads;
       later, they paved the way for her
on the river-path

as she washed her hands
       of their billowing
eyes.

Chants for Type: Beamboy Watching Cartoons in Five-Star Hotel Room Eating Ice Cream

(Denounce after me:)

Capitalism marxism stealing accountantism board directorism

(Now denounce:)

Mother loss father cross stepbrother dross brother toss

(Now I won't refill the vanilla. You carry the tub.)

More brother step moss loss mother toss father. Cross?

(Chessboard through head you must think on. Revolver shot. Bang.)

Cross chess brother head, bang board. Father moss. More.

(Mother vision floats in white figure. Cartoon flails into dumpster.)

Ha ha head bang white ha ha bang chess head mess moss.

(Toilet flush muffle. Employer zips pants, laughs. Bugs Bunny runs into rathole.)

Tom Jerry cherry merry mess step less mother less bang less white

(Traffic lights reflected on window pane. High-rise shadow. Disco Ilamai 90.5 FM hoarding.)

Merry light dance light strobe light boss light mother light. Hoard light whole light.

(Channels flip through violet flecks. Woman dances, yellow dress flaps.)

Whole merry light strobe, boss! Mother light. Light light. Bang light. Mess light.

(Inane wind carries broken feather to woman. Bugs Bunny shoots out. Spoon scrapes tub.)

Cherry feather weather hoard mother whole father hole

(Brotherly pat as employer catches flung remote, reduces treble. Bass mass bunny scampering.)

Brother bunny whole cherry!

(Employer parts curtain. Looney logo appears. Unsated Beam flips to woman, now in bunny dress, points.)

Cherry bunny?

(Tub rattles into wastebasket. Voile slinks back. Employer strokes phone cord, asks catch my point?)

Clearly You Are ESL: Workbook Cursieve III

There is a well full of water.

_____.

The girl has an empty pot.

_____.

The mother works at the stove.

_____.

The father waters the fields.

_____.

The stove is burning.

_____.

The water is cold.

_____.

The girl fills the pot with mud.

_____.

The father's hands are muddy.

_____.

The mother wipes her hands.

_____.

The field is full of muddy water.

_____.

The mother burns the rice.

_____.

The girl breaks the pot.

_____.

The rice is boiling.

_____.

The father breaks her hand.

_____.

The mother is burning.

_____.

The girl's eyes water.

_____.

The rice is in the mud.

_____.

Notes

"Watchman": Kongu refers to a region in Tamil Nadu, which often covers Coimbatore and surrounding areas. Meen refers to fish. Kovai Sarala is a popular Tamil actress who often plays supporting roles.

"Two Corruptions...": Bappi Lahiri is a music director who worked with Mithun Chakraborty and created the legendary soundtrack for Disco Dancer, a movie which catapulted him to fame and solidified his status as a dancing superstar.

"Eye Prints": This poem was made as a response to Pakistani artist Sophia Khwaja's "call" and the narrative I focused on was resistance as well as ideas of nationhood that emerge within popular culture, particularly against or in support of the nation state. I collaged from two primary texts, *Last Letters: Prisons and Prisoners of the French Revolution* by Olivier Blanc, which I found at the Mason library sale, and from the comment boards on Rediff. com. Material from the first text is on the left side, and from the second source is on the right side of the page.

"Catalog of Pronouncements...": Ellis Road is an interior road that runs between Royapettah and Mount Road, and was the location of the Asian College of Journalism (ACJ) where I studied journalism. Bukhari or Buhaari is a famous restaurant, and Standard Biscuit Factory is (or was) a snack/bakery/onfectionery shop on Mount Road. The Amman or Goddess temple I refer to was located close to the ACJ building.

"How the Webs Came to Be...": This poem is based loosely on hoardings of Sivaji, which was one of Thalaiva or Superstar Rajinikanth's most successful films in the 2000's. The phrase "shut up da somberi" is not his dialogues per se, but a dialogue attributed to him by a Hindi commercial (several of which started to reference Tamil words after the release of this film and created a "meme" of sorts); "karuppu thaan enakku pidicha color-u" is a Tamil song from the film *Vetri Kodi Kattu* that references Rajinikanth as the ultimate Tamil icon. The line "Thalaiva Supershtar" is a reference to the titles that are given to Rajini, and I use the "sh" sound because I have heard Rajini himself pronounce "s" as "sh" on occasion in his films. The very last line "dei keLava" may also be pronounced, alternatively, as keZhava and is a pejorative term used to refer to older men; if I remember correctly, a minor character in the film was referred to using this term. Zari is a kind of embroidered strip of cloth used in all kinds of attire in India, including sarees and men's tunics/ kurtas.

"Yama's Buffalo...": Yama is the Hindu god of death and is depicted as riding a buffalo. Avial is a vegetable stew that is popular in Kerala and some parts of Tamil Nadu as well. Pogaielai is an alternative spelling for "pogai-ilai," the Tamil word for tobacco.

"Picked up Episodes": Koovathur is a coastal village/ town not far from Chennai, India; it has acquired a reputation as a resort/ beach destination now; however, in 2006 or so, when this poem was written, it was developing fast; at the time, real estate was at a premium. Mahabali refers to the "asura" (demon) king who is celebrated all over Kerala during Onam. The myth of Mahabali also links him to Vishnu's Vamana avatar; the Brahmin youth asks Mahabali for a boon (three "steps" worth of land) to which Mahabali agrees. Having encompassed the whole of the material world (the heavens and earth) with the first two steps, the Godhead turns to the king, who is said to have offered his own head as the space where the youth could put his foot down, finally. This dominant narrative is contested by Bahujan narratives where the idea that Mahabali is an "asura" king is dismissed and the myth rejected.

"Mariaatha": Mariamman or Mariaatha is one of the most common forms of the Mother Goddess worshipped in Tamil Nadu. In popular culture, she is depicted as someone who protects women and keeps the pox and other diseases at bay.

"Chants for Type: Beamboy...": The word "beamboy" refers to "Bheem boy," the burly bodyguard for Madan, played by actor Kamal Hassan, in *Michael Madana Kamarajan*, a Tamil film made in the 90's. The bodyguard, played by Praveen Kumar Sobti, also concurrently played Bheem in the Mahabharat series aired on Doordarshan. The character is portrayed as someone who is strong but simple and likes to watch children's shows, particularly cartoons, in his spare time.

About the Collective

The (Great) Indian Poetry Collective is the coming together of poets who believe words can transform lives. Founded in 2013 in Bangalore, India, as a not-for-profit press, the Collective publishes innovative, diverse poetic voices from India and the diaspora. Through a mentorship model, members of the Collective support one another in producing beautiful poetry books as well as workshops, readings, and community and school events.

Poet Advisors

Carolyn Forché
Ranjit Hoskote
Prageeta Sharma
Arundhathi Subramaniam

Also from The (Great) Indian Poetry Collective

Geography of Tongues by Shikha Malaviya
Bountiful Instructions for Enlightenment by Minal Hajratwala
Histories of the Future Perfect by Ellen Kombiyil
The Trouble with Humpadori by Vidhu Aggarwal
Slow Startle by Rohan Chhetri
Bird of the Indian Subcontinent by Subhashini Kaligotla
How Many Countries Does the Indus Cross by Akhil Katyal
Terrarium by Urvashi Bahuguna

www.greatindianpoetry.org

Ranjani Murali has an MFA in Poetry from George Mason University in Fairfax, Virginia. She teaches composition and literature courses at Harper College, Illinois. Her first book of poems, *Blind Screens*, won the *Almost Island* inaugural manuscript prize and was published in 2017. This is her second book of poems.